King Donal's Secret

Story by Malachy Doyle
Pictures by Richard Watson

OXFORD
UNIVERSITY PRESS

In a cottage in a forest in a time long ago, a young girl called Morna lived with her mother. Every evening, as the sun was setting, Morna went down to a clearing, where she would sit by the river and listen to her beloved birds. Her favourite sound was the song of the nightingale, whose music rang through the woods long after all the other birds had fallen silent.

The only thing that spoilt Morna's joy was fear of the King's men.

"When they ride, you hide!" her mother always warned her. "Or you may never be seen again!"

The King's name was Donal, and there was one thing he was very embarrassed about. His ears were so big that he would allow no one to see them, for he was sure that if they did, they would laugh at him.

Every time he passed a group of children, he imagined them singing, "Donal the King has donkey's ears! Donal the King has donkey's ears!" So he always wore a thick purple hood over his head. He wore it by day and he wore it by night, and he only took it off twice a year, when his hair was to be cut.

The King had another problem. He could not use the same barber more than once, for fear they might spread the word about his ears.

So, as soon as his hair had been chopped off, he would throw the unfortunate barber into jail, and that was that.

One day Morna and her mother were out collecting wood in the forest, when the King's guards rode by.

"Run!" cried the old woman, but it was too late. Although she cried and protested, one of the guards grabbed Morna, pulled her up onto his horse, and galloped away.

The guards took Morna to the King's palace.

"I am sorry, child," the King told her, "but there are no more barbers left in the land. Everyone hides when I send my men out to find someone to cut my hair. Now that you are here, I am afraid that I shall have to ask you to do it."

"As you command, Your Highness," said Morna, for she knew that she had no choice. "But first I would like to say a proper goodbye to my mother, for I did not have time when your guards stole me away."

The King admired the girl's courage and agreed, for he was not a cruel man, just rather foolish. So he called for his horse, Morna climbed up behind him and, as dusk fell, they rode off into the woods.

Morna's mother cried when she saw her daughter again.

"She is my only child and all I have left in the world. Please let her stay here with me!" she begged the King.

The King felt sorry for the poor woman, but someone had to cut his hair, so what could he do?

Morna hugged her mother tightly, before pulling away. "I must go with the King," she insisted. "There is no other way."

It was almost dark by the time Morna and the King made their way back to the palace.

They passed through the clearing, where Morna used to listen to the birds.

"Can we stop here for a minute, Your Highness?" she asked. "This is my favourite place of all and I should like to sit here, one last time."

The forest was silent, for night was falling, but suddenly the air filled with song.

"Listen to the nightingale!" cried Morna. "It is the most beautiful sound in the world!"

The King tried to listen, but he could not. "I can hear nothing," he said.

"That's because you always cover your head!" said Morna, laughing. "Pull down your hood and you will hear it."

King Donal was afraid to uncover his ears, but he really wanted to hear the most beautiful sound in the world, so he pulled back his hood.

The bird's song poured in through his ears and into his heart, and he wept.

"I had no idea there was such beauty in the world," he said.

"Are there other things that I should hear?" the King asked Morna, as they arrived at the palace.

"Many things, your Highness," she told him. "But they are not all beautiful, like the nightingale."

"What do you mean?" asked King Donal.

"You do not hear the crying of the poor," said Morna, for she had often watched them from the edge of the forest. "They come here every night, begging for scraps from your table, but your guards turn them away."

Later that night, King Donal sat down to feast with his lords. The tables were piled high with food and drink, as always, but the King stood up before the meal had begun and asked everyone to leave. Then he removed his hood.

At once he heard the cries of the poor people at the gate, desperate for food, just as Morna had told him.

Covering his ears once more, for the sound was too awful to bear, he summoned his guards.

"Open the gates!" he ordered. "Let the poor and the hungry share my meal!"

He called for Morna. "Thank you, child," he said, "for helping me to listen to my people. How could I not have heard them before?"

"Maybe you did not want to," said the girl. "Or maybe it was your greedy lords who did not want you to because they wanted all the food for themselves."

"Is there anything else I should hear?" asked the King.

"Yes, Your Highness," the girl replied. "I think you should hear how your lords talk about you behind your back."

She led him to the room where the men had gathered. The door was slightly open, so the King took down his hood and listened, unseen.

The lords were very angry that he had spoiled their feast.

"Why should the poor people have all the food, instead of us!" one cried. "It is not right! We cannot allow it!"

"Let us get a doctor to say that the King is mad," said another. "Then one of us can take his place!"

"Why don't we go to war with another country!" suggested a third. "The King can lead all the poor people off to fight, and we can stay here and have a feast every night."

"You evil men!" cried King Donal, rushing in. "Throw them all in prison!" he ordered his guards.

"But we can't," the guards replied. "The prisons are all full of barbers."

"Release the barbers, then!" roared the King. "Make them all into lords, instead!"

The next day Morna cut the King's hair.

"I think it is good to have big ears," he said, admiring himself in the mirror. "For it means I can hear my people."

"Yes, it is good, Your Highness," said Morna.

"Thank you, child," he told her, when she had finished her work, "for helping me to find wisdom at last. Now you may go back to your mother."

From that day on, King Donal ruled wisely and well. No one laughed at his enormous ears, for everyone was content and fear had left the land.

At last they had a king who would listen, to pain and to greed and to beauty.

And every evening, he would ride into the forest to meet Morna, and to hear the beautiful song of the nightingale.